I'm Grace Elliott, a Scotswoman living in France at the time of the French Revolution. (My boyfriend was the cousin of the French king, Louis XVI. He supported the revolution but it didn't do him much good—like many aristocrats, he ended up having his head chopped off by the guillotine.) I supported the king and became a spy to help the royal family. I got thrown into this miserable prison after helping another aristocrat to escape the mob. The diary I'm writing is later published as a book, *My Experiences in the Revolution*, in 1859. I survive the revolution (just about) and die a wealthy woman in 1823.

Author:
Jim Pipe studied ancient and modern history at Oxford University, then spent ten years in publishing before becoming a full-time writer. He has written numerous nonfiction books for children, many on historical subjects. He lives in Dublin, Ireland, with his lovely wife Melissa.

Artist:
David Antram was born in Brighton, England, in 1958. He studied at Eastbourne College of Art and then worked in advertising for fifteen years before becoming a full-time artist. He has illustrated many children's nonfiction books.

Series creator:
David Salariya was born in Dundee, Scotland. He has illustrated a wide range of books and has created and designed many new series for publishers both in the UK and overseas. In 1989 he established The Salariya Book Company. He lives in Brighton with his wife, illustrator Shirley Willis, and their son Jonathan.

Editor: **Stephen Haynes**

Editorial Assistant:
Mark Williams

© The Salariya Book Company Ltd MMVII

No part of this publication may be reproduced in whole or in part, or stored in a retrieval system, or transmitted in any form or by any means, electronic, mechanical, photocopying, recording, or otherwise, without written permission of the publisher. For information regarding permission, write to Scholastic Inc., 557 Broadway, New York, NY 10012.

Published in Great Britain in 2007 by
The Salariya Book Company Ltd
25 Marlborough Place, Brighton BN1 1UB

ISBN-13: 978-0-531-18745-6 (lib. bdg.)   978-0-531-13927-1 (pbk.)
ISBN-10: 0-531-18745-4 (lib. bdg.)   0-531-13927-1 (pbk.)

All rights reserved.
Published in 2008 in the United States
by Franklin Watts
An imprint of Scholastic Inc.
Published simultaneously in Canada.

A CIP catalog record for this book is available from the Library of Congress.

Printed and bound in China.
Printed on paper from sustainable sources.

You Wouldn't Want to Be an Aristocrat in the French Revolution!

Liberté, égalité, fraternité, ou la mort!

Written by
Jim Pipe

Illustrated by
David Antram

Created and designed by
David Salariya

A Horrible Time in Paris You'd Rather Avoid

Franklin Watts®
An Imprint of Scholastic Inc.
NEW YORK • TORONTO • LONDON • AUCKLAND • SYDNEY
MEXICO CITY • NEW DELHI • HONG KONG
DANBURY, CONNECTICUT

Contents

Introduction

You are Grace Elliott, a Scotswoman born in 1754. Brought up in a French convent in Edinburgh, you are known for your great beauty, your style, and your wicked ways! One of your brothers is so fed up with your bad behavior, he tries to kidnap you. You escape to London, where in 1784 you meet Philippe, Duke of Orléans. He falls for your charms, and two years later you're living in Paris together. Philippe is rich and powerful, a cousin of the French King Louis XVI. You get to hang out with French aristocrats (posh and rich!).

Bad luck! This is not a good time to be rich or famous. In 1789, revolution breaks out in France. Angry peasants roam the countryside, burning castles and killing aristocrats. It's even more dangerous in Paris. If the mob doesn't get you, the guillotine will. You soon realize why you wouldn't want to be in the French Revolution. Don't lose your head!

People live in fear of the guillotine, a machine for chopping off heads!

Blame It on Louis

As mistress of the king's cousin, you soon become popular at court. But meanwhile, outside the palace walls, trouble is brewing. Many aristocrats, including Philippe, are fed up with the way France is being run. Other people are fed up because the nobles own all the land and get all the best jobs. The peasants are *really* fed up because they can barely afford a loaf of bread.

Unfortunately, King Louis XVI is a weak, foolish ruler who is bossed around by the queen, Marie Antoinette. The queen comes from Austria, France's enemy, so no one trusts her. Philippe hates her!

Reasons to Hate the Royals

Louis walks like a peasant!

UGLY KING. Louis is short, fat and very nearsighted. He's also greedy. For breakfast he wolfs down four veal cutlets, a whole baked chicken, six eggs, a slice of ham, and one and a half bottles of champagne.

Oui, oui!

Can't you wait?

THE BIG HOUSE. People are jealous of the magnificent palace of Versailles. If only they knew! It looks great on the outside, but inside, the palace is filthy. The smell of human waste in the corridors would make you sick!

BOREDOM. Marie Antoinette is utterly bored at court. To keep herself amused, she likes to ride a donkey in the Bois de Boulogne or play at being a milkmaid. That's no way for a queen to behave!

The royal palace at Versailles near Paris is famous throughout Europe. It has more than 1,000 fountains in its gardens.

Handy Hint

Whatever you think of the royals, be careful what you say. When the Marquis de Pelier whistled at the queen in 1786, he was thrown in prison for 50 years!

The queen has skin like a peach!

Yes, it's all yellow and hairy!

I want to be king!

I can see why!

JEALOUSY. The king's brother and Philippe think they could do a better job of being king. The prince is also jealous of the king's marriage to the gorgeous Marie Antoinette.

Money Troubles

Life at court is just one long party, but Louis XVI has big money problems. He has spent a fortune helping the Americans fight the British during the American Revolutionary War (1775–83). Queen Marie Antoinette continues to spend, spend, spend. By 1789, the government is penniless. Louis tries to raise taxes from the aristocrats. When they refuse, he has to call France's parliament, the Estates-General, for the first time in 150 years.

BIG SPENDER. The queen splurges on towering wigs, fine clothes, and jewelry. Her new portrait makes people angry because of her expensive outfit.

Life at Court

TOP SECRET Learn the language of the fan to send secret signals to your friends.

WORN OUT. After hours of partying, ladies need to be in full ball gowns by 8 a.m., ready for Mass in the chapel.

In 18th-century France, people rarely wash. Use strong perfume to mask your own smell, and powder your hair to absorb grease.

I should hope so. This dress cost you a fortune!

OVER THE TOP. Everyone wants to be noticed by the queen. One young aristocrat wears a pink and green waistcoat, blue satin breeches, blue and red stockings, a lemon and green striped overcoat, and an enormous wig.

The Peasants Are Revolting

Just for Fun

While the peasants live in misery, the queen plays at being a milkmaid in the palace grounds. She has two cows, a flock of perfumed sheep, and... servants to do all the work.

While you and Philippe enjoy a life of luxury at court, peasants all over France are starving. When bread doubles in price, riots break out. In parliament, the aristocrats refuse to meet with the common people. The commoners are locked out of the meeting chamber, but they swear to stick together until Louis listens to them. Louis finally gives in. He forces the aristocrats to join with the commoners in a new parliament, called the National Assembly.

Coochie coo!

Who'd Want to Be a Peasant?

POOR. Peasants are forced to pay taxes, while rich nobles and bishops pay nothing. If the peasants protest, the army is sent to kill them.

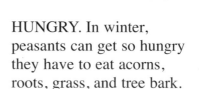

MISERABLE. Peasants share tiny mud huts with their animals. Most have only one set of clothes and wooden shoes. Terrible plagues wipe out family and friends.

HUNGRY. In winter, peasants can get so hungry they have to eat acorns, roots, grass, and tree bark.

PICKED ON. Landlords kick peasants out of their homes. Tax collectors beat them up. Peasants can't even trap the rabbits that nibble their crops!

Storm the Bastille!

Everyone hopes that the National Assembly will solve France's problems. Then, in July 1789, the king sacks Jacques Necker, a popular minister. Bad move. Angry crowds gather in the streets of Paris. On July 14 they go on a rampage and attack the Bastille, an old prison that is a symbol of everything they hate. The army joins in. They blast open the gates and the Bastille surrenders. The king no longer controls Paris. Many aristocrats flee the country. Others accuse Philippe of starting the riot, but you manage to convince them that he was away on a fishing trip at the time.

Don't speak ill of the dead!

He always was a bit stuck up!

Heroes or Horrors?

The Bastille was described as a horrid place. Yet prisoners wore fine clothes, brought in their own beds, and ate and drank well.

FAMILY DAY OUT. Writers tell how little children picked up used cannonballs, then dodged back under cover to hand them over to soldiers attacking the prison.

No Chance

When the commander of the Bastille surrenders, the mob drags him through the streets. They scream and spit at him so much that he asks to die. "No problem," says the mob, stabbing him with knives and swords. Then they chop off his head and stick it on a pike. Worried? You should be...

FREEDOM! Ninety-eight people died during the attack to rescue just seven prisoners. The leaders parade around a thin prisoner with long white hair to show how the prisoners have suffered.

The Great Fear

I t's a revolution! Even the dim-witted Louis realizes just how bad things are. Three days later he travels to Paris. Dressed as an ordinary citizen, Louis announces that he is now "King of a Free People." The cheering crowds believe him.

Then rumors spread that aristocrats are hiring armed gangs to destroy the harvest. Angry peasant mobs attack and burn castles and manor houses. Victims are strung up on lampposts and their heads stuck on pikes. Philippe, who supports the revolution, changes his name to "Mr Equality." He is popular with the mob, but this doesn't make you feel any safer.

Come on, boys, time for a bonfire!

Liberté, égalité, fraternité, ou la mort!
(Liberty, equality, fraternity, or death!)

What Is There to Fear?

TRAITORS. Republicans—those who want to get rid of the king—claim that their rivals in the Assembly are being supported by foreign kings. Soon everyone is accusing everyone else of being a traitor.

Traitor!

I said it first!

What have I done?

SECRET POLICE. With a network of informers, innocent people are imprisoned without trial.

INVASION. There are fears of invasion by Spain, England, and Sweden. Many think the Austrian king, Joseph II, will invade to protect his sister, Marie Antoinette.

SCAPEGOATS. Rumor has it that door-to-door salesmen are poisoners, and that aristocrats are using galley slaves to attack peasants. People start hunting for the "GAL" branded on their backs.

FALSE ALARM! Panic starts when people think they see a building on fire—but it is just a red sunset reflected in the windows.

Vive la Révolution!

When word gets out of a lavish banquet at Versailles on October 5, 1789, a crowd of 6,000 hungry women march on the palace to demand bread. They break in and force the royal family to return to Paris, where they are shut up in the Tuileries Palace.

With the king a prisoner in the palace, the National Assembly removes many of the harsh laws that made people so angry. But you're still worried—where will it all end? You become a spy for the queen, taking messages to the Baron de Breteuil, who is organizing an escape plan for the royal family.

Learn to Fit In

It's safer to pretend to be a revolutionary—especially now that you are a spy.

FLY THE FLAG. France has a new flag, the *Tricolor*, made up of red, white, and blue stripes. If you don't have a flagpole, drape the flag from your window.

RED CAPS. Revolutionaries wear red caps made from soft felt or wool. They are like the caps worn by freed slaves in Rome as a sign of their freedom.

Oh, it'll be OK, be OK. Hang the nobles from on high! Oh, it'll be OK, be OK!

SING SONGS. Revolutionaries love to sing rowdy marching songs. *Ça Ira* (above) is very popular—make sure you learn it.

Handy Hint

Get a revolutionary haircut to blend in.

Short, straight hair—Oui! Bravo!

Long, curly hair —Non! Too posh.

LONG PANTS. The city mob is called the "sans culottes" ("no breeches"). They wear long, stripy trousers instead of knee breeches, which are a sign of wealth.

I'm starving. I could eat a horse!

She looks nice and plump!

The Escape

In June 1791 you help the royal family escape, but they are captured and brought back. Paris erupts in anger. Some of the Assembly want to get rid of Louis XVI. Others want to go to war with Austria and Prussia to stop them coming to the king's rescue.

In April 1792, war is declared—but the French army is in shambles. As the Prussian army advances toward Paris, the mob turns nasty. On August 10, 1792, it storms the Tuileries Palace. In a ferocious battle, 1,200 guards are killed. You escape, but the royal family are flung in prison, and on September 21, the French Republic is created.

Do you think they've seen us?

No, but they'll hear us if you don't keep quiet!

How Not to Escape!

Louis XVI plans to escape to the Netherlands. Once there, he hopes he will get support from Austria and return with an army. But his escape is a disaster.

SLOW COACH. The queen insists that the family travel together. This means using a larger, slower coach.

Handy Hint

Don't stick up for the royal couple. A cook's assistant who defends the queen is fried in butter, then burnt alive by the mob.

DOESN'T ADD UP. There are six people instead of five listed on the passport. Duh!

BRIGHT IDEA? The escape is planned for June 20, one of the shortest nights in the year—not a good idea when you need the cover of darkness.

CHICKEN? Louis refuses to let his bodyguards use their guns.

Liberté, égalité, fraternité, ou la mort!

SHUSH! Louis takes two rest stops and chats with passersby as if nothing unusual is going on.

SNIFFED OUT. The royal family are disguised as servants, but the queen's expensive perfume blows their cover.

Mob Rule

While you remain in hiding, the Prussian army continues to threaten Paris. Thousands of young men flock to join the Revolutionary army. Their leader, Georges Danton, encourages them to be even more daring. The mob take this the wrong way. They rush into the prisons, killing 1,400 prisoners.

Though the French army defeats the Prussians, a general mood of panic remains. The Assembly is replaced by a new parliament, the Convention. Two groups, the Jacobins and Girondins, fight for control.

The Jacobins use the mob to attack their enemies. They persuade the Convention to execute the king. From the balcony of your house, on January 21, 1793, you hear the roar of the crowd as the king's head rolls into a basket. Nine months later, the queen is executed too.

Heads You Lose!

THE ROYAL FAMILY. When Louis XVI's head is cut off, people dip their pen tips in his blood. Locks of his hair are sold as souvenirs.

When a fleeing aristocrat knocks on your door, you hide him in the gap between the mattress and the springs in your bed.

Keep your head down!

Don't worry, I'd like to keep it exactly where it is—on my shoulders!

ARISTOCRATS. Madame de Lamballe's head is stuck on a pole and paraded past the queen's window. The sight turns the queen's hair white.

PRIESTS. Hundreds are killed because the Catholic Church supports the king.

CRIMINALS. Thieves are dragged from their cells and chopped up by the mob.

Handy Hint

If they catch you, you *might* be lucky. Mademoiselle de Sombreuil saves her father's life by drinking a glass of blood. Ugh!

Political clubs spring up all over France. One group, led by the "Red Priest" Jacques Roux, is known as the "Angry Ones."

The Terror

In 1793 the Jacobins replace parliament with a 12-man "Committee of Public Safety." Their leader, Robespierre, believes that creating terror will make France strong. Over the next year, thousands are sent to the guillotine, including many of your aristocratic friends.

You are sick with worry and grief. When soldiers find a letter in English in your house, you're arrested as a spy—as is Philippe, despite his support for the revolution. No one is safe. When people in the Vendée region rebel against Paris, Robespierre shows no mercy. Hundreds of rebels are drowned or buried alive.

All Change

With Robespierre in charge, nothing is sacred!

What month is it?

I haven't the foggiest.

CALENDAR. The months are given new names such as Foggy, Windy, and Flowery. Weeks are now ten days long, creating only three weekends a month—not very popular!

Look who's here! Two more whose heads can roll!

NAME CHANGE. People must call each other "citizen" instead of "monsieur" or "madame."

Hello, citizen.

Hello, citizen.

Handy Hint

Don't hoard soap or sugar, or you'll be sent to the guillotine. Even the king is accused of hoarding bottles of rum.

CHURCHES. The churches in Paris are closed. Many others are looted. Donkeys are led through the streets dressed as bishops.

ARMY. All single men aged 18–25 must join up. Many injure themselves to get out of it.

Bubble Trouble

Some brave people fight back against the "Committee." On July 14, 1793, Charlotte Corday visits leader Jean Paul Marat. Marat has a skin disease, and is lying in a cool bath to stop the itching. Pretending to hand over a list of traitors, Corday stabs him with a kitchen knife. Marat is given a hero's funeral. Corday is sent to the guillotine.

Madame la Guillotine

The Committee is ruthless. Once all their enemies are locked up or killed, they turn on their own supporters. When the mob complains about food shortages, its leaders are executed. In Lyon, even the executioner is given the chop. In all, 40,000 people are killed. The guillotine certainly speeds things up!

You, meanwhile, rot in jail, sharing a cell with Madame du Barry, the elderly mistress of the king's father. She is executed in December 1793, only weeks after Philippe, Duke of Orléans. It will soon be your turn!

Don't worry, you won't feel a thing!

CHOP, CHOP. The guillotine is a quick way to kill people, but the blood-soaked scaffold makes the executioner slip. Railings are built to stop him falling off the platform. In Nantes, the guillotine is painted red so the blood does not show.

A HEAD FOR BUSINESS. Madame Tussaud follows the executioner's wagon to the graveyard and makes wax masks of the rich and famous. She tours the wax heads around Britain for 30 years, then sets up her famous waxworks in London.

SPECTATOR SPORT. Victims are carried in a wooden cart past jeering crowds. Many come just to watch. In the front row sit groups of women who knit or nurse their babies while watching the heads roll.

Handy Hint

When watching an execution, remember to hold your nose. The rotting blood under the scaffold smells terrible.

Famous Last Words

EAGLE-EYED. As he is about to be hanged, the Marquis de Favras is handed his death sentence, written out by a court clerk. "I see," says the Marquis, reading it over, "that you have made three spelling mistakes."

SHIVER! Jean Bailly is the first mayor of Paris following the 1789 revolution. It doesn't save him from Robespierre. While Bailly awaits the guillotine, a spectator shouts, "You're trembling!" Bailly replies, "Only from the cold, my friend."

HEY, GOOD-LOOKING. Danton is sentenced to death by Robespierre. "Make sure you show my head to the mob," he tells the executioner. "It will be a long time before they see its like."

WHOOPS! On the scaffold, Marie Antoinette accidentally steps on the executioner's foot. Her last words are, "Pardon me, monsieur."

Down with the Tyrant!

Just when you think things can't get any worse, Robespierre brings in a new law that helps him to execute even more people. Soon even the Committee realize the Terror has gotten out of control. In July another 1,300 people are executed. Worried that they will be next, some of the Committee plot against Robespierre. On July 27, 1794, he is met with cries of "Down with the tyrant!" from the Committee.

Robespierre is arrested, and on July 28, 1794, he and 21 other Jacobins are executed. Soon after, you are freed from prison. You have survived the Terror, unlike so many of your aristocratic friends.

Will the Real Robespierre Step Forward?

SQUEAKY. Robespierre has a squeaky voice that turns into a howl when he is really angry. When he first speaks in the Assembly, everyone laughs.

DOG-LOVER. Robespierre likes to take long walks around Paris with his great hound, Brount, who keeps guard at his master's door each night.

You can't arrest me! I run this country!

Handy Hint

Don't cross Robespierre! When Danton said of him, "I doubt that man has the sense to boil an egg," he was sent to the guillotine.

Big Head

When soldiers come to arrest him, Robespierre tries to shoot himself, but the bullet only smashes his jaw. His head won't fit under the guillotine, so the executioner rips off the bloody bandages. Ouch!

A SIMPLE LIFE. Robespierre is honest and hardworking. He lives on coffee, water, bread, and oranges. Despite his power, when he dies he is only worth $15.

NO TO DEATH! As a young lawyer, Robespierre resigned rather than sentence a murderer to death. Yet this same man sent hundreds of innocent people to the guillotine!

The End of Revolution

The Terror is over. The country is ruled by a group of five men known as the "Directory." A young general, Napoleon, helps the Directory defeat its enemies. By 1799 he is one of three men running France. A year later, he's in complete control. Napoleon organizes the country's laws and sorts out its money problems. The revolution is over. Phew!

Soon you are back to your old pleasure-seeking ways. Rumor has it that you turn down an offer of marriage from Napoleon himself. You die a wealthy woman in 1823, at the ripe old age of 69.

A FRESH START. Life in Paris returns to normal. The streets are filled with rich young aristocrats. Many nobles rebuild their estates. Despite the revolution, the poor are still poor, and the peasants are still hungry.

VICTIMS' PARTIES. Only those with a close relative killed by the guillotine are invited. Ladies wear a thin red velvet ribbon around their neck, to mimic the bloody slice of the guillotine.

FICTION. The Terror became the setting for some great stories. *The Scarlet Pimpernel*, written by Baroness Orczy in 1905, tells the story of an English spy who uses cunning disguises to save French aristocrats from the guillotine.

In 1804, Napoleon crowns himself emperor.

I could have been empress, but he's a bit short for me.

RETURN OF THE KING.
Louis XVI's eight-year-old son, Louis-Charles, is taken from his family and kept in a damp, flea-infested prison, where he dies from illness in 1795. His 15-year-old sister is handed over to the Austrians later that year. However, the king's brother returns to the throne as Louis XVIII, after Napoleon's defeat in 1814.

Glossary

Aristocrat A member of the nobility.

Bastille A prison in Paris, destroyed during the revolution. Nothing is left of it now.

Breeches Tight-fitting, knee-length pants worn with long stockings.

Citizen The title by which republicans addressed one another.

Guillotine A machine for beheading people, named after Dr. Guillotin, who thought it was the best way to execute enemies.

Jacobins The most successful group of French revolutionaries.

Liberté, égalité, fraternité, ou la mort! Liberty (freedom), equality, fraternity (brotherhood), or death! —the slogan of the revolution.

Louis XVI The king of France at the time of the revolution.

Marie Antoinette Louis XVI's queen, sister of the king of Austria.

Parliament A group of people who meet to make laws and decide how a country should be run.

Peasant A person who does farm work, growing just enough to live on.

Plague A highly contagious disease, spread by rats and fleas.

Prussia A country that is now part of Germany.

Republic A nation that is ruled by elected leaders instead of a king or queen.

Republican A person who thinks that his or her country should be a republic.

Revolution The overthrowing of a government by the people.

Revolutionary A person who supports a revolution.

Sans culottes A nickname for a French revolutionary. It means "no breeches"; they wore loose-fitting pants instead of breeches.

Terror The time during the French Revolution when large numbers of people were executed.

Tricolor The red, white, and blue flag that has been the national flag of France since the revolution.

Tuileries A royal palace in Paris, now destroyed.

Versailles A huge royal palace near Paris, now open to tourists.

Index